OUR CHILDREN'S YEAR OF GRACE

Considerations for Use in the Home-School by Parents Who Wish to Teach Their Children to Live Throughout the Year with Christ and His Church

By Therese Mueller

Foreword by the Very Rev. Martin B. Hellriegel

"Thy children shall be as olive plants 'round about thy table."
from the Gradual of the Nuptial Mass.

Martino Fine Books
Eastford, CT
2018

Martino Fine Books
P.O. Box 913,
Eastford, CT 06242 USA

ISBN   978-1-68422-244-5

Copyright 2018
Martino Fine Books

Cover Design Tiziana Matarazzo

Printed in the United States of America On 100% Acid-Free Paper

OUR CHILDREN'S YEAR OF GRACE

Considerations for Use in the Home-School by
Parents Who Wish to Teach Their Children to Live
Throughout the Year with Christ and His Church

By Therese Mueller

Foreword by the Very Rev. Martin B. Hellriegel

"Thy children shall be as olive plants 'round about thy table."
from the Gradual of the Nuptial Mass.

PIO DECIMO PRESS
Box 53, Baden Sta.   St. Louis 15, Mo.

Nihil Obstat: WILLIAM J. FISCHER, Censor Librorum.

Imprimatur: JOANNES J. GLENNON, Archiepiscopus Sancti Ludovici.

TABLE OF CONTENTS

Paulina,   December 2021

"Truly I tell you, unless you
change and become like
little children, you will never
enter the kingdom of heaven."
                    ~ Matthew 18:30

3

God Bless your family.
                    Love,
                        Leslie

FOREWORD

The world awaits a new order. Those that are not of this world pray for the blossoming of the ancient, yet ever new order inaugurated by the Prince of Peace and Saviour of the world at 3 o'clock on the first Good Friday afternoon.

This Christ-order means: The LIFE, LOVE and PEACE of Christ, bequeathed by our Divine Head to His Church, His Mystic Body, His extension, His fulness. The more consciously and intimately we live with the Church, the more we shall possess this order of Christ in our lives and homes.

The purpose of this small, but great book is to pave the way for a closer, holier and more vital union of the Home with Christ and his Church.

The author, Dr. Therese Mueller, has drawn from her triple treasure-trove: her Catholic Faith, her Catholic education and her Catholic home-life. What she suggests she practises and lives with her truly Catholic and inspiring family.

No father and mother, no preacher and teacher can read "Our Children's Year of Grace" without being drawn deeper into the "Year of Grace," the Christ-Church-year, whose purpose is to build up the order of Christ: The LIFE, LOVE and PEACE of Christ, who is Teacher, Savior and King of the world.

And by being drawn deeper into the order of Christ, we shall become restorers, builders and apostles of the order for whose return we long and pray: "Thy Kingdom come!"

MSGR. MARTIN B. HELLRIEGEL.

St. Louis, Missouri.
Feast of St. Callistus, the lover of Christ's Order.
October 14th, 1943.

THE ADVENT SEASON

ADVENT

With the beginning of a new year of grace, we parents face the responsibility of keeping our children in close touch with Mother Church, for she shows us the way to a fuller understanding of the sacred mysteries of our religion, wisely represented and celebrated in the course of the liturgical seasons.

Then let us use in the "mother school" or "home school" everything that helps our children to understand and to penetrate deeper into their faith. There must be no exclusion of the little ones, for they are still so near to the wisdom of paradise that they often express things in simple ways more clearly than we do with many words.

So we tell the children that Advent means arrival, coming, and emphasize that it stands first of all for the approach of the promised Messiah, and secondly for the return of the ascended Christ at the end of the world. Both thoughts are expressed in the liturgy of the Advent and Christmas season, including the feast of Epiphany, which not only celebrates the revelation of the divinity of Christ (through the adoration of the magis, the baptism by St. John and the miracle at the wedding in Cana), but also the final revelation of his Kingship in the last judgment.

On the Saturday evening before the first Sunday of Advent we wind a wreath of evergreen, pine needles, cedar branches, or holly, large enough to hold four red candles, equally spaced, and suspend it with four red ribbons (or purple ones if the candles are white) tied on the spaces between the candles. We prepare the branches, cut them to the desired length, attach the candles to a piece of round wire or reed, and then do the winding and finishing in the living room, while we talk to the children about the meaning of the symbol: The circle represents the unceasing flow of sun years or the sun itself following its prescribed course; the candles divide it into time, which we can measure and count—four of them for the thousands of years of waiting for the arrival of the Savior, remembered on the four Sundays of Advent, as we prepare for Christmas, the birthday of Christ. They represent also the thousands of years mankind is waiting for his second and final coming,—called by Christ himself "a little while." The finished wreath we hang in the living room at a suitable place, where it can be seen by all.

Then we open our missal and study the text of the Mass for the first Sunday of Advent. And we reflect on the fact that the season of Advent means more than the birthday of the child of Bethlehem, more than just a sentimental remembrance. For the King of Eternity is beginning his work of salvation by becoming man, and by dying on the cross; and continuing it by being with us every day in the sacrifice of the Mass—yet fulfilling it not earlier than the last day of time, when he re-arrives as God *and* man on the clouds of heaven, as lightning appearing from the east to the west, with great power and majesty.

As death is the only door through which we can enter into eternal life, so the day of judgment and destruction of this world is the only way that the work of our salvation can be perfected, that we can come into the glorious possession of the ever-lasting kingdom of Christ. And as we should learn to love and should teach our children to love the day of death so we should also bring ourselves to hope and long for the second coming of Christ with the same eagerness and readiness as the world waited for his first appearance.

On Sunday evening under the light of the wreath we recall all that we studied and worked over the night before, the Collect and the leading thoughts of the Epistle and Gospel. We sing our Advent hymns, and especially the "Rorate Coeli," which after some practice will become an essential part of our family prayers.

From the missal we choose a few ideas for each Sunday.

First Sunday: St. Paul's exclamation "now is the hour to rise from sleep. To put on the Lord Jesus Christ" (two very impressive pictures to children of all ages.) Gospel of the end of the world.

Second Sunday: St. John the Baptist, the great saint of Advent, in the testimony of Christ, the Angel to prepare the ways of the Lord. Preparing the ways of the Lord is also our task, every day, but especially in the Advent season.

Third Sunday, Gaudete: Rejoice in the Lord, for the Lord is nigh! Keep your hearts and minds in Christ our Lord—teach-ings of St. Paul's letter to Philemon. Communion Antiphon: . . . take courage and fear not: behold our God will come and save us—a consolation for those who do penance. Gospel: the voice of St. John crying in the wilderness, giving testimony of Christ: the one in the midst of you whom you know not. Do we know him or do we not?

Fourth Sunday: St. John again raising his voice in the wilderness. "Prepare the way of the Lord, make straight his paths. Every valley shall be filled and every mountain and hill shall be brought low" . . . Again the picture of building a road. Let the children work it out with drawing pencil or clay—they will never forget the meaning!

On the three Ember days in the third week of Advent the Church shows us three great pictures to contemplate on: the Annunciation, the Visitation and St. John the Baptist crying in the wilderness. Let us fill these with as much life and understanding as we can and then let the children in their simple, but direct manner play these mysteries—not as a "show," but as a vital expression of their living in them. The less stage and costume required, the more likelihood that only piety and real affection will lead the play. Acted prayer—that is what it should be, and what children like so much and sometimes do so beautifully.

In the very beginning of Advent the Church celebrates the feast of St. Nicholas, the great bishop, seafarer, father of the poor and friend of children. So great was his regard for the welfare of his flock, that in time of a famine he rigged out a ship to buy wheat in a far off country; returning to haven after a heavy and dangerous sea, he delivered the wheat to his starving people, but kept enough to bake "sugarbread" as a treat for his little friends. He was so concerned about each one of his flock, that he is said to have thrown a purse with money in it through the window of a young girl, too poor to get married. The legends are countless, which deeply admiring centuries wound around his picture, and any time since the fourth century, when he lived in Myra in Asia Minor, there were countless followers imitating his example of considerate and unselfish charity among the poor and the children. It is St. Nicholas who teaches us all about giving and sharing and surprising. Let us then in the spirit of St. Nicholas plan our Christmas giving, transferred from his feast to that of Christmas only because on that day we celebrate the Feast of the most generous and the most abundant of all givers, God the Father, Who gave us his only begotten Son. Only if our gifts are compatible with the spirit of St. Nicholas and worthy to lay beside the crib of Bethlehem, will they be real Christmas charity.

THE CHRISTMAS SEASON

THE VIGIL OF CHRISTMAS

The Advent time (in the narrower sense) is at its end: the anniversary of the arrival of our Saviour in the flesh gives us a right and a cause for joyful remembrance and celebration. His arrival in glory is still to come—who knows when?—and the Church's thought of that Advent is woven like a red thread into the liturgy of the season. Let us be aware of that.

"This day you shall know that the Lord will come and save us: and in the morning you shall see his glory." This word from the vigil Mass is like a preface written over a Christian's life: this day you shall know, tomorrow you shall see. The short night of death only separates our knowing from the glorious seeing and experiencing of the eternal glory in God and with God.

In the narrower sense, however, this word should give our Christmas vigil its face, its character. All happiness, all joy that the Holy Night is holding for us, is sealed in it like a rose in the bud—and is not the rose-bud before the full blooming the symbol of high beauty? It is a day of preparation. Let us plan this day so, that at least our being busy with the material things does not use up our time and our energy entirely.

CHRISTMAS

There will be a quiet hour in the light of the four candles of the Advent wreath. This seems a little more appropriate than the current custom of having the tree dressed and lighted several days before the Holy Night. I am often tempted to ask people who have their Christmas decorations up so early if they have also begun to eat the holiday turkey and their Christmas candy. (And it might be added, the practice of singing Christmas carols weeks ahead of time is a bit premature. Surely, there are plenty of good Advent songs!) Let us give everything its proper time, and the proper time for the lighted Christmas tree is Christmas Eve and not earlier.

And after we look back over the blessed time of expectation — Israel's, the Church's, ours—we lead the children out of the Advent atmosphere into the "Christmas room," where we have prepared the crib and the tree and the things we choose as the expression of our Christmas joy and generosity and love for each other: the presents to represent the present of all presents, God's only begotten Son as an infant in the manger, Jesus who became our brother.

Whatever the traditional time of our Christmas celebration in the home is let

10

us take care, that the numerous presents do not distract our and the youngsters' mind from the celebration at the crib: singing together, reading the Christmas story, that is, the Gospel from the shepherd's Mass, followed by the Collect and the beautiful Lesson from St. Paul's letter to Titus: . . . we should live soberly and godly and justly in this world, looking for the blessed hope and coming of the glory of the great God and our Saviour Jesus Christ . . . And then after parents and children have wished each other a blessed Christmas and the graces of the Holy Night, comes the time for exchanging presents.

Since the time of Saint Francis of Assisi people have built the stable of Bethlehem in their churches and homes. Generation passed unto generations a pious heritage of more or less artistic statues and grottoes, and more than that, the knowledge of how to make them and build them into the living room as an essential part of it. We know of Tyrolean wood carvers who start with the first Sunday of Advent to erect the widespread scenery of Bethlehem and Jerusalem; we heard of a wise mother, who nourished her children's Christmas longing with an "every day a surprise" plan: each day in Advent she let them find a little something, which belonged to the crib, building it up slowly, but retaining—of course—the holy family until Christmas eve.

Cribs in the home have become far too rare a sight in this country and it seems as if the "village" to be found under almost every Christmas tree is but a poor remainder of the "little town of Bethlehem" of our forefathers. (It is tragic that the centerpiece, the essential part got lost, and the stage, the accidental, took over and assumed the whole space). It is not too late for us to replace what has been lost. All year round we can tinker and collect for the crib that will be the real center-piece of our Christmas decoration. We might even make the statues ourselves—perhaps especially the statues, since those sold in stores are deplorably unworthy and without dignity. You will be surprised how satisfying it is to make something your-self, make something which will be of honest material and reflect the dignity of personal work. Any kind of statues, whether carved in soap, wood or plaster, cut with a jig-saw from flat board and painted, made from clay or with wire and cotton and dressed in cloth—will be better and more dignified than all mass-products. A broken bushel basket once served as our stable, the truest we ever had as shelter for our hand made statues. Let us never be ashamed of poverty, since it was Christ who chose poverty for his birthplace! And if we start right now we might have the holy family next Christmas, the shepherds following in another year, growing with our crib until the three kings with their whole train are present.

11

This is not liturgy, you say? But it is. It is the representation of St. Luke's Christmas Gospel—from the worried arrival of Mary and Joseph after the vain search for an inn, the first adoration by the holy couple, the annunciation in the fields, and the coming of the shepherds, to the solemn procession of the three kings who were on their way all the time, to adore the King of Kings on Epiphany.

The liturgy, then, which we study night after night before the crib, sees to it that we do not "get lost" in the concentration on the childhood of our Saviour, calling our attention on the day after Christmas to the great martyrdom of St. Stephen, the Deacon, who died praying for his enemies. On the third day is the feast of St. John, the Apostle, "whom Jesus loved." A beautiful custom in some old countries is the "drinking of St. John's love" on that day. Wine, blessed with a special blessing and prayers is served in the home before the main meal: the father lifts the cup toward the mother. "I drink you the love of St. John;" she having answered: "I thank you for the love of St. John," drinks to the eldest child and so on, including guests and servants. The simple beauty of this ceremony gives character and dignity to our family supper too, especially if there is a John in the family, who celebrates the day of his patron saint. A similar custom has been connected with St. Gertrude of Nivelles.

Holy Innocents. This is the day when we mothers fight back our tears and Mother Church is donned with the vestments of mourning. However, the infant martyrs triumphantly turn the day into a feast for the children. From their glory all infants receive glory, from their innocence innocence. Many a pastor invites on that day the "infants and sucklings" of his flock to church, that they may "perfect the praise of the admirable name of the Lord" in their own manner and language and after that he dismisses them with a special blessing. In convents and schools the youngest becomes "superior" or "principal" for that day—why should not we in the family too, give some credit to the youngest child on account of the innocent martyrs, giving them a say as to what is to be sung and prayed, eaten and played.

EPIPHANY

In like manner we meditate on the deep meaning of all the feasts of this season: Circumcision, Holy Name, Holy Family, until on the eve of Epiphany we change the arrangement of the crib: making room for the arrival of the three magis or kings,

12

carried in solemn procession by the singing children to adore the King of Eternity, and to offer their symbolic gifts.

Let us plan this feast-day carefully, so that it regains the glory it had in the olden times (the glory it still has in the liturgy!), when it was not only equal, but even superior, to Christmas. With the calling of the gentiles (and as we are the gentiles), we celebrate gratefully our being called with the wise men to the adoration of Christ. We are called to be not only witnesses, but even the tools by which his divinity is made manifest to the members of his mystical body, to each baptized person. This is not only the greatest experience of our life but also our most obliging responsibility.

To restore everything in Christ! In the light of the mysterious star which led the three kings from their far away countries and tribes to the crib in the stable we see even the things of our daily use in a new light—at least our forefathers did, when for them Epiphany was the great day of blessings in the home. The blessing of the homes often is given by the pastors from the parish church door or in the church steeple in the four directions if the parish is too large to go from house to house. If the time is made known to the parishioners, the family could gather around the home-altar or the crib. While the pastor performs the rite over all the houses of his parish, the father would say the prayers and psalms of the blessing, going through all the rooms of the house, blessing them with holy water.

Gold and frankincense are blessed in church in memory of the symbolic gifts of the wise men; gold to be offered for sacred vessels in the parish, incense to be burnt in the home if we wish, during our family prayer. Blessed chalk is distributed to the parishioners that they may write over the lintels of their doors the initials of the three kings with the number of the "anno Domini": 19 K ✝ M ✝ B ✝ 45, reminding all who enter and leave through that door, that we too should be ready as they were to leave everything, and to follow the star of the Nativity. We also must profess the divinity of Christ, his kingship before an unfaithful Jerusalem, an unhospitable Bethlehem.

Three main sources of our daily food also are included in the liturgical blessings of Epiphany: bread, eggs and salt are blessed after the morning service and eaten with the holiday meals. Let us ask our priests to renew these beautiful blessings. We can at least reverently pray and perform the rites in our "Church at home," with the father reciting the prayers.

13

Epiphany, the word, means arrival, appearance, revelation. Remembering the first revelations of Christ's divinity, the liturgy turns our eyes to the second Epiphany, his Advent, when his divinity is made known "to all flesh," when he appears on the clouds of heaven. Not the birth in the stable, not the tidings of the angels— given to a few simple shepherds only—but the splendid and strange train of the three kings from the orient, who publicly asked for the new-born King, so they might adore him—made it known to all folk in Jerusalem and Bethlehem, that this Child is more than poor people's son.

Twelve years later the doctors in the temple heard words of divine wisdom from this young boy, as he answered their questioning. But many years later at the baptism in the Jordan, the heavens opened and the voice of the Father came forth like thunder: this is my beloved Son . . . and the Holy Ghost hovered as a dove over him. (Gospel of Octave of Epiphany). This manifestation of his divinity was made before a large crowd, and St. John the Baptist "gave testimony that this is the Son of God." And still another proof there was of divine power in the "son of Joseph," when at the wedding at Cana he revealed himself in the first miracle. (2nd Sunday after Epiphany). "He manifested his glory and his disciples believed in him." Then we see the growth of his power and glory, his love and his kingdom Sunday after Sunday; until the also rising hatred of his enemies casts a shadow of the cross—in order that there might be a victorious Easter morning.

CANDLE-MASS

Yet before we enter through the dark gate of Septuagesima into the Easter sanctuary, we have the beautiful feast of Candle-mass or Purification, with another procession in the home, since children and all that are childlike at heart, so love them.

In the early morning we bring the candles to the Church to receive the blessing— one candle for each member of the family (including one for an expected child or godchild to be his baptismal candle) and the two candles we keep always ready for the administering of the Holy Eucharist in our home.

The rite of the blessing and the prayers of the procession are so beautiful, that we should repeat them at home in the evening, when the family members, who could not attend the morning service are present. Each one carries his own candle lighted— Baby's is put in a safe place and burns too—so we go singing and praying, led by the

14

father of the family, through all our rooms, blessing them and our life and work in them for the coming year. "Hear thy people, O Lord, we beseech thee, and grant us to obtain those things inwardly by the light of grace, which thou grantest us out' wardly to venerate by this annual devotion." (Prayer preceding candle procession).

The candles can be used often; not only on sick days, in sorrow, or temptation, but on all feast days, anniversaries, name days, and before important personal decisions.

The symbolism of light is one which the Church uses constantly in her liturgy. Why should we not, too, make frequent use of this beautiful symbol in our homes?

THE LENTEN SEASON

THE PERIOD OF PRE-LENT

With the Saturday before Septuagesima Sunday we enter the period of remote preparation for the celebration of the Easter-mysteries. By sharing the passion and cross of Christ—only by sharing the passion and cross—shall we be enabled to partake in full of the glory of the resurrection. And this resurrection with him and in him is the very goal of our life.

In motherly wisdom, therefore, Holy Church introduces us to the forty days of Lent, in a gradual manner, so that we are prepared even by the changing color of vestments and the very tone of the liturgical services, for the earnestness of the Quinquagesima.

The Christmas song, "Gloria in Excelsis," is henceforth allowed only on feast days. The "Alleluja," angel-given exclamation of enthusiasm and jubilation, sung in numerous tones so frequently in the liturgy of the Mass and the Hours, is silenced entirely.

Reviving an old custom we make a farewell celebration of the Alleluja, singing it in all the tones we know from the year 'round before we "give it up," the first Lenten sacrifice. Denying ourselves the most perfect expression of jubilation in our prayers, we are enabled to retreat deeper and deeper into the spheres of penance and self-abnegation. (Many weeks from now there will come the great moment when the deacon approaches the Bishop with the words: "I announce to you a great joy: it is the Alleluja." And the priest sings it in three different keys before the gospel of the Holy Saturday Mass, the choir repeats it jubilantly, and we all rejoice again: "Alleluja: Glory be to him who is.")

Septuagesima Sunday. Two parables in today's Epistle and Gospel make our introduction of Lent to the children easy: the one, of the race—each one has to run so that he may receive the crown, and must prepare for it in all conscientiousness; and the other, the story of the householder and the workers in the vineyard. God it is who gives us our place in the vineyard, whether our work is to bear the heat and burden of the day or to have the short hour before nightfall.

Sexagesima Sunday. St. Paul in today's letter to the Corinthians tells us of the burden he had to carry. "My grace is sufficient for thee," he was told. May it be for us too. We are to be a field for his seeds, open, willing; God will do the plowing, will send rain at its time—and the fruit must be a hundredfold. Fortunate are those of us who live near to the soil which is now being prepared for the spring seeding. Watching the work in field and garden we compare what is done outside with the work waiting to be done within our souls.

Quinquagesima Sunday. The epistle on charity is sufficient to contemplate on for a lifetime. How beautiful a prelude to the Lenten season! In the Gospel Christ himself foretells his passion—are we too among those who did not understand what he said? Are we too blind? Then let us cry out with the blind man, that our eyes may be opened.

In countries with pronounced Catholic traditions and culture these three days before Ash Wednesday are carnival days, a time of plenty in food and fun and pleasure. Something like that should also take place in a Catholic home, as it is good psychology to experience and enjoy what we intend to "give up" (think of the Alleluja farewell!) and helps much in a right start for Lent.

That does not prevent our having a solemn and silent procession through the house, to gather the old palm from pictures and crucifixes. Carefully—because it is a sacramental—we burn it as a lesson on the "dust" we are and to which we must return. It means much to the children if they can burn their own piece of palm as an expression and confirmation of a Lenten resolution they made. However let us take care that their resolutions (and ours) are not just negative "give-ups," and "do-aways," but positive "build-ups," overflowing from a new abundant charity and love requiring outward expression. So is fasting only one factor of Lent, needing the compensation of prayer and good deeds—both of which rank even higher, since there is no dispensation for these.

Let us also see that the little (or big) "pharisees" take the advice of Jesus himself, and not look for a reward from men. There is too much boasting about "giving up candies, and movies, and cigarettes"—the children get the impression that they are growing a visible halo because of these external things. Suggest to them that they make of it a secret offering to the Most High, known only to themselves and their parents.

THE LENTEN SEASON

Daily Mass is the real "Lenten sacrifice," and the studying of the daily Mass formula on the evening before is the best means to lead us the way the Church wants us to

19

go. Work out together one or two thoughts that can be easily remembered the next morning and during the day. Let us remember that the Church has two ideas woven into the Lenten liturgy: the preparation of the catechumens for baptism on Holy Saturday, and the reconciliation of sinners and their atonement. We prepare for the renewal of our baptism; we suffer with Christ for our sins; we are buried with him in penance so that we may rise with him to a new life in grace and glory.

The Sundays of Lent are meant by Mother Church as a pause on the hard way. They are a measure of relaxation and reward for our effort, in order to gather new strength for the coming week. Especially the "Midfast," the Sunday Laetare, is full of joyous anticipation of a victorious Easter day, since in nature by that time the sun has already conquered the darkness and the cold, and spring has driven out winter. Let us foretaste the coming Feast, and let us rejoice that we have reached and conquered half of our steep way.

PASSIONTIDE

Passiontide centers our thoughts and prayers around Christ the Son of Man, the Agnus Dei, sacrificed for us. Palm Sunday is another "Children's Day," the day when children marched waving their palms and singing jubilant "hosannas" in Jerusalem. Let the children therefore be present at the blessing of palm and the procession in the church, let them walk around proudly with their blessed palm through the house, adorning each room with the new palm. Let us all have a little palm cross on our dress or coat to remind us all through Holy Week that we must carry our cross in patience if we wish to share Christ's glorious Easter victory. To find all the hidden treasures in our Missal, a whole lifetime is too short. And yet each year we should draw from this fountain eagerly, as if we would exhaust the whole depth.

During the Paschal Days themselves surely we can do no better than to urge our children to participate to the fullest in the services of Holy Mother Church. They are so profound and absorbing that even young children early learn to love them.

Easter housecleaning is more than just a custom: it can be an outward reflection of the inner newness of soul. But it should be planned carefully so that it does not intrude into the Holy Days and disturb the recollection and concentration of the family during this holy time.

The sacred liturgy of Holy Thursday will unfold in all its splendor and magnificence in the bishop's church. Whenever it is possible it might be good to attend these services in the cathedral. The mandatum (maundy) alone—which is often only celebrated in cathedral churches and monasteries—is a great spiritual experience. And to witness the consecration of the holy oils will, for once, make us "diocese-minded," uniting us with all those who are to receive—for life or death, for strengthening or healing—the sacred oils. The naturally more elaborate, more solemn presentation of the liturgy, together with the strong language of the mighty cathedral architecure, will never fail to impress us deeply and lastingly.

We should emphasize simple meals during this week. Some day we shall have one of only unleavened bread and wine. On Holy Thursday, however, there is occasion for a more elaborate meal since the Christian meal has always been sacramentalized in its relationship to the Divine Banquet instituted on this day. And it can be begun or climaxed with singing the beautiful "Ubi Caritas Et Amor," made even more meaningful if there are guests.

But there is a note of simplicity to all that is done during the week: there should be hours of silence, spiritual reading and explanations of the Church services, to "bring home" the spirit of the day. Where it is possible the family, especially the older members, may attend the "Tenebrae" on Wednesday, Thursday and Friday evenings. This powerful drama of the forsaken, betrayed, crucified Bridegroom was composed by Mother Church for us to take part in, and the dimming of the candles to express the abandonment by the disciples one by one surely relieves any "monotony" for all but the youngest children. Even they feel rewarded if Christ's Resurrection is expressed by a loud clamor, and not by the feeble sounds our so "refined" civilization tends to make.

Having attended Holy Week celebrations in many different places, I am surprised to discover how strong a part memory plays. For each day, for each rite there is one outstanding experience of the past, which as it were, bursts through to the present. For instance, I shall never forget one adoration of the Cross on Good Friday in a large city parish.

The priest had explained that our coming up to venerate the cross should not be just an act of pious compassion but a solemn expression of our willing and abiding acceptance of our life's cross. "Since not everyone is expected to receive Holy Communion," he said, "so you are not all expected to solemnly confess this readiness." For minutes the congregation was in deep silence. Then, finally, a few old people and young children stepped forward to lead the way. What followed was the most sincere procession I have ever witnessed. This was adoration "in spirit and in truth."

And then, one "Exsultet" twenty years ago in my home parish has never been excelled. To me it was the very "discovery" of this great hymn; and this experience rings through each Exsultet I have heard since—and perhaps, if God wills, through the one I want to pray at my life's end.

Experiences like these will all the more convince us that we should build in our children a similar wealth of experience that cannot be destroyed by rust or dust.

Holy Saturday is the baptismal feast of the Church. In the evening, before the preparation for the morrow's great Sacrifice, we have a solemn renewal of our baptism—all members of the family united. Baptismal robes and baptismal candles should be displayed at the home-altar. Then follows the renewal of the baptismal vows, a song of praise and thanksgiving for having received the gift of life. With the new Easter water the father blesses each member of the family and the whole house—and the garden and the fields if we have them. (The children will be proud to bring home the holy water from the Church. It is well to have a special container for it, fittingly decorated with symbols of the sacrament of Baptism or of the Trinity. The material required is merely an attractive bottle and enamel paint.)

With the confidence that we are ready to participate in the re-enacting of the resurrection we thank God for the grace of a Holy Lent, a sacred spring.

THE PASCHAL SEASON

PASCHALTIDE

Easter Sunday is the day for our biggest celebration. With joyful enthusiasm we prepare the home. There must be flowers and green for it. Let the imagination of all the members of the family be used so that the long kept back jubilation may break forth with freedom. Whether we string oranges or paint eggs with appropriate symbols of the season, or cut out in golden letters the "Alleluja" and the "Resurrexit" to bedeck the dining room, the effect will be good, and symbolic, the work of our hands. The Church desires that Easter shall have the dominant place of the year, and we must work to that end. (Christmas with its crib and tree is quite a competition in the minds of our children!)

The mother's concern is above all, with the "centerpiece," the basket of bread and eggs, Easter roast, cake and sweets and fruits, all carefully arranged to be blessed by the father, when the family returns from the participation in the paschal meal of the Eastermass. Formerly these things were taken to church, and blessed by the pastor, who together with the poor of the parish, received a share from its content. We hope that it will not take another generation to restore this beautiful custom. In the meantime we content ourselves by reciting the prayers of this blessing ourselves. The head of the family reads them, the others answer, and thus the Easter-meal is reconnected in a special way with the sacrificed and victorious Paschal Lamb received at Mass—an echo of the old Christian "agape," wherein was expressed the unity of all members in their common Head, Christ.

It is easy to understand why the Easter eggs—the egg is the symbol of life in every language and culture—are carefully painted with the symbols of Christ, his resurrection and victory. The early Christians themselves used the symbol of the cross over the circle, expressing the Redeemer's triumphant victory over the empty grave. The chicks and bunnies used today, though of a lower rank, also serve a good purpose, because they suggest new life, spring, and fruitfulness, especially to the smaller children.

The magnificent "Exsultet" from the Blessing of the Eastercandle, repeated before our baptismal candle on the home altar; the alleluja sung according to all the tunes we know; the Sequence from the Eastermass, the long-missed Gloria, the Regina Coeli—all these add up to a beautiful and impressive Easter devotion in the family circle.

24

Let us not forget that the Church celebrates the Redemption for eight full days, so that we will not be among those who came to Mass frequently during Lent only to stop abruptly on Easter Sunday. (Mass is still "penance" for them, and the time for penance is over! The reason is that they are not aware of the beautiful Mass texts for the octave.) All during the week we continue therefore each evening to explain to the children, and to meditate with them, on the Mass propers of the succeeding day. This fills us with their high beauty, their fragrance of the final blossoming of all things at the end of time, in, through, and with the glorified, risen Christ.

Then the octave day of Easter, the Sunday in "albis", will not find us low-spirited, down in some lower region of Christian living. ("Low" Sunday—what a "low" name for a day so "high" in fame!) On the contrary it will find us on the elevated plain that stretches from the empty grave to the mountain of the Ascension, walking with Christ and his Apostles for forty glorious days, days without fear and hate, days with happiness and paschal cheer.

ASCENSION

On this day two currents flow through the soul. There is the happy knowledge that Christ, our Brother, has ascended to the right hand of the Father to prepare eternal dwellings for us, and yet on the other hand there is the painful realization that he whom we loved has gone from us, leaving us alone in a hostile world, a world which for us holds no better fate than it did for the God-Man, now "First-born from the dead."

To us, too, is the angel sent: "Why wonder you, why are you looking up to heaven. There is no time for staring at heaven whither he has gone, no time now for wondering. Work rather that he may find you and the world prepared for his coming on the great Day. For you are not left behind as orphans, but rather are you filled with Christ's Spirit, the Paraclete who will stay with you until the end of the world."

After keeping faithfully the Rogation days, giving our prayers and hopes and petitions to the ascending Victor of Golgotha, with Mary and the apostles we join hopefully in the novena of preparation for the coming of the Holy Spirit. Our need for him is extreme in this hate and blood-filled time. The "Veni Creator" sung in Latin or English to the choral melody is added to our family night prayers, and we carefully explain it to the children, verse by verse.

PENTECOST

Pentecost is not "just another Sunday," but the second culmination, the highfeast that concludes the Easter celebration. Another task is therefore ours,—to find a worthy expression of it in the home. The symbol of the Holy Spirit (a simple folding cut in red craft paper) dominates the home altar, and red roses are blooming in our backyards now to glow radiantly beside it, symbols of love and devotion. (One time we tried to express the Introit: "the Spirit of the Lord hath filled the earth", in simple silhouettes. Under the dominating dove with the seven gifts streaming forth from it, we arranged the symbols of the universe, from sun and moon to the monsters in the depths of the sea. It expresses the blessed assurance that there is no sphere in the universe which is hidden or cut off from the unceasing activity of the Spirit of the Lord. Deo Gratias.) Let us listen to the Voice of him who breathes where he will: in restored nature, in the prayer of a child, on the battlefields of the world.

On the eve of Pentecost we gather for a two-fold celebration: the birthday of the Church and the anniversary of our "personal Pentecost," confirmation. Solemnly we vow love and faithful obedience to her, our Holy Mother, through Christ our Lord, who in the hour of the death of Christ went forth from his opened side as the new Eve, mother to all that are born from the water and the Holy Spirit. On Pentecost for the first time she opened the locked doors of the "upper room," she was made known to the great multitude of pentecostal visitors in the Holy City, as chosen by Christ and fortified by his Holy Spirit to bring the message of the Redemption to all mankind, until time is no more.

Then we recall the day when we were confirmed with the Spirit of the Lord, the day when we were sent forth by the bishop to testify for Christ in our everyday life. We repeat what happened and what was said to us on that great day and ask God to renew in us the grace and power of our confirmation.

Send forth thy spirit and they shall be created and thou shalt renew the face of the earth, alleluja, alleluja!

THE TIME AFTER
PENTECOST

THE SUNDAYS

The field has been prepared (pre-Lent), the seed has been sown (Lent), we experienced the glorious resurrection of the dead grain (Easter), we witnessed its growing, and at the "fullness of maturity" the Spirit of the Lord came to it in the fruitfulness of pollen, (Pentecost). Now we are patiently waiting and watching for the growing and ripening of the fruit, for the great day of harvesting with Christ in his glory.

Mother Church's colors are green, as the fields and the meadows, strewn with the white flowers of virginity and the red ones of martyrdom. Like the land-man Mother Church keeps on praying for sunshine and rain, for the best for the souls and bodies of her children, that they may ripen full and fair, worthy to be gathered into the eternal barns.

Sunday after Sunday she leads her children to the fountain of eternal life, so that they may eat and drink their daily need of grace and divine help toward the final goal. Each Sunday is a "Little Easter," a re-enactment of the great mystery of resurrection from death, of new life out of the supreme sacrifice. With our brothers from the early days of the church we must stress, concentrate on the one highfeast, celebrated over and over again on "the first day of the week," we must make it the center of our religious life as well as of our recreation (re-creation!!) in the spiritual as well as the physical sense.

To give ourselves, our life and love, our sorrow and cares, our soul and body, our wishes and fears into the hands of the Father—"through Christ our Lord"— that is what we are expected to do and in return we will be filled with the abundance of Christ's grace and love and perfection. We will be transformed over and over again into "other Christs," we will be united with him, who gloriously overcame suffering and death, who is awaiting us to give us part in his glory, after we share his suffering here on earth.

As we make each Sunday a "little Easter," let us give to each Saturday something of the spirit of "Holy Saturday"; an atmosphere of happy preparedness and peaceful expectation of the coming day of the Lord. That is a real family task and worthwhile to work for. Whenever I am lonesome for the home of my childhood, it is the "air" of the "Sunday Eve" I am longing for; the smell of soap and wax and fresh linen, of a simple one-dish-meal mixed with the promising odor of the cake for the morrow, the tip-toeing through the "best rooms," locked for us children during the week. "Moses take off your shoes, the place you are standing on is holy" my father used to say, often with a smile we did not see—to us it was just too true. It was as if the whole house was alive with the expectation of something great and beautiful—almost as wonderful as the Sunday itself!

Let us try to "steal" some hours from the approaching Sunday to make our minds and soul ready, to "tune in" as the church bells of my home town did, spreading peace and happiness over the roofs of the old city—as Mother Church does, when she anticipates Sunday with the Vespers on Saturday evening.

It is up to us to create a new "Sunday cult," an atmosphere in which our children will grow up to a deeper, more religious understanding of the day of the Lord.

THE FEASTS

The time after Pentecost is abundant with special feasts: of our Lord, of his Mother, of his perfected brothers and sisters: the Saints.

All the Feasts of the Church Year depict for us the shining Light of our salvation, viewed as through a prism. In the many colors are the varied mysteries of our faith, the life and death of Christ, and the life and death of those, who, while still on earth, were transformed by Christ-in-them—now enjoying a heavenly communion with him.

The Feast of Corpus Christi. Holy Thursday in glory and joy. This is the feast of the first Mass, feast of the Eucharist, feast of the sacramental Christ, who lives, works, suffers and dies with and in each one of us, among his brothers and sisters still laden with the hundredfold burdens of life. That they may understand it better, let us tell the children of the Corpus Christi celebration in many Christian countries, where the Hidden God is carried about the fields and streets, through villages and cities, accompanied by the singing and praying faithful who carry banners and flowers and sacred symbols; along ways covered with green and flowers, adorned with garlands and posters; by houses decorated with holy pictures, candles, flower-decked windows and doorways; with the four big altars for solemn benediction built right into the living quarters, or set up in the fields, carefully prepared by the whole neighborhood. What a grand experience it is to go around with the Lord in his triumph, showing him where our family, our friends, our co-workers live! How thrilling to be one of a great multitude following him!

The Feast of the Sacred Heart. The texts of the Mass alone on this day are sufficient to correct the "too-human" attitude we have toward the Sacred Heart, the soft, sentimental, feministic air we project on the image of the most holy, most virile love (divine and human), that was ever embodied in any heart. Mother Church leads us to the Cross (grown-children and small-children) where the Sacred Heart is pierced with a lance, after having suffered the death of all flesh to redeem all flesh from death. Here is the best Sacred Heart picture, one that does not allow senti-mental feelings of romance and sympathy, but impels us to reverence, co-offering, self-abandonment, sacrifice. In such a picture we see Christ bleeding from countless wounds, healing the wounds of all centuries. There is no room here for false mysticism or cheap glamor.

The Feast of the Most Precious Blood. (July 1.) The Church emphasizes on this day the redeeming and healing power of Christ's Blood, shed once and for all time, for all mankind, and all generations—the Most Precious Blood that fills daily the hundred thousand chalices on the altars of the Church.

The Feast of the Transfiguration. (August 6.) We are given a glimpse of the splendor and beauty that is waiting for us too, after we have shaken off the garment of our mortality. Like Peter, James and John we too would like to build our tabernacles—but the time of our probation is not yet fulfilled. Gratefully rejoic-ing in the knowledge of our calling to share the splendor of Christ in eternity we go on to fulfill our mission in life.

The Feast of Christ the King. For the time being we have to fight his fight against the powers of evil and darkness, we have to suffer at the hands of his enemies, —but in the end we know that victoriously he will come "on the clouds of heaven" to judge the world; to take home his faithful servants to the eternal banquet. The Lord is King—even when he dies like a "criminal" on the cross. He is King now and for all history, though his followers be many or few, for his majesty and dignity do not need our recognition of them.

From the Feast of his Kingship it is but a short time to the Last Sunday of the liturgical year, when the gigantic picture of his final coming on the day of judgment is put before our eyes. The world is in ruins, living and dead are awaiting the verdict, in terrible majesty his Kingship is evident from one end of heaven to the other—to the joy of those who believed, to the horror of those who denied and blasphemed.

Interwoven with the feasts of our Lord are feasts of our Lady.

The Visitation. (July 2.) This is the touching feast of love and charity between the two holy women blessed with the knowledge of the mystery of the Incarnation; the feast of the Magnificat (which should be prayed more often in the family.) Let it be a real Mothers' Day and show the children their part in it. Do we know an expectant woman, who materially or spiritually needs our visit, to help her with her work, to prepare in any way for the arrival of the coming child? Let us go there and serve her, as Mary went to serve her cousin Elizabeth.

The Great Day of the Assumption of Our Lady. Although in this country we may have to work on this day, at home at least, the spirit of a holy day can prevail, with all that belongs to it. Let us all rejoice and be lifted up by the glorious mystery of the elevation of the soul and body of the Mother of God, to the Queenship of Heaven.

On a rural vacation in my childhood I learned how great a feast Assumption Day is—should be, and I bitterly regretted that I was a child of the city where no one seemed to know about the blessing of wild herbs and flowers in memory of the "lilium convallium", the lily of the valley (as the Canticle of Canticles calls the Bride of God.) For days the children had hunted through hills and fields to find the traditional number of wild-flowers (from 20 to 40 species) which they carefully bound into a big bouquet. When before the High Mass the herbs were lifted by their proud owners—to catch at least one drop of Holy Water—it was as if hills and woods and fields had entered the church to testify about the empty grave of Mary. And before dusk the families had distributed the blessed herbs between house and stables, pantry and fields and gardens so everything was united in the blessing that flowed down from the Blessed One made Queen of Heaven.

Are we of the city too proud to admit our poverty and how much we are in need of this very beautiful sacramental? Will we be humble enough to bring the fruits of our garden, our find of wild flowers from backyards and vacant lots to the blessing at church?

31

The Feast of the Nativity of our Blessed Mother (September 8), of the Holy Name of Mary (September 12), of the Seven Sorrows (September 15), of Mary's Motherhood (October 11), the Presentation of the Child Mary in the temple (November 21)—all should be celebrated at home with hymns and psalms and a little while of contemplation on the story and the spirit of the day.

The Feasts of the Saints. There are more Saints in heaven than stars in the sky—but how little we know about them! Why not have a Saint-of-the-month study club at home? By choosing one Saint, and gathering painstakingly whatever information we can find about his life and work, we will be able to picture him to our children, making him very live and real. And because it is fascinating, the title will soon become the Saint-of-the-week.

By **All Saints' Day** then the "heavenly host" will be alive with well known and beloved faces, not only of the patron Saints of the family but of many more who have contributed to our religious growth.

All Saints—how many of our forefathers and foremothers are among them? Whether or not we know their names and number, we know that they are one with us. (Some of them may not have yet arrived at the eternal glory: it is our filial duty to help these through Purgatory so that they may be all together around the eternal banquet table—where we one day hope to join them.) The litany of the Saints, said or sung, will soon be a favorite of our family, and for a change we may say a litany of all the patron Saints of the family members, whom we should greet every day.

All Souls Day is the proper time to make us and ours acquainted with the liturgy of death, the office of the dead. Even children can feel the majestic, earnest and consoling hope that swings in its every verse. During the rest of November we can tell more about the theme: death, its inevitable certainty, its character as punishment, its transformation and sanctification through Christ's victorious death on the cross. Let us tell the children stories: of how Saints died and how sinners, how great men and women of history, how our own grandparents and relatives left this world of misery for the eternal fields of glory. We are strangers in this world, our true home can never be here. Christ's kingdom is not of this world. But we pray and work that his kingdom come, and his glorious Advent on the clouds of heaven.

The ring is rounded again. A year of grace and growth is fulfilled. God's charity may grant us another. Grateful and humble let us start anew.